Sanna Myrttinen

The Adventures of Feliz

Feliz Finds a New Home

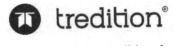

www.tredition.de

Verlag und Druck:
tredition GmbH, Halenreie 40-44, 22359 Hamburg

ISBN
Paperback: 978-3-347-35261-2
e-Book: 978-3-347-35262-9

To everyone out there in search of their path in life.

Prologue

Once upon a time, far, far away, nestled in the valley of a remote mountain range, there lived a group of peace-loving dog monks. They spent their days contemplating the secrets of the universe and the mysteries of cats, practicing compassion, and wagging their tails.

A few times a day, howling could be heard for miles away, echoing through the trees and bouncing over the mountaintops, as the canine friars chanted themselves into elevated states of doggy bliss.

As fascinating as it would be to stay here and follow the daily lives of these unusual spiritual seekers, it is time we move on. Our main character, an elderly dog monk, is about to release his current form, rejoin his doggy ancestors and be reborn onto Earth as a little Petit Basset Griffon Vendeen by the name of Delice – not as a monk, this time around, but with the mission to guide a young woman to a life of deeper meaning, inner peace, and joy.

Where It All Began

Deep in Småland, in the heart of Southern Sweden, stood a solitary, red farm, surrounded by green fields and gently rustling birches. Visitors and day trippers strolling by were alerted to the inquisitive, barking Basset Griffons who reigned supreme on the farm. "Ah…," thought the old dog monk, "the perfect, welcoming place to make my entrance as Delice."

On this particular summer evening, just as the farm's human inhabitants were enjoying a little break from their thirteen puppies, a sharp howl split the evening air. Startled, the family followed the sound out to the barn. Looking around, they tried to locate the howl, until they almost stumbled over their youngest female dog and realized she was its source! There, in the high grass, lay Cherie, protectively cleaning her two newborn puppies.

The family could not believe their eyes. They already had two big litters from different mothers - and now Cherie?! Hadn't the vet just been around to guarantee that their teenage lass, who had barely graduated from being a puppy herself, was not pregnant? That her playful and flirtatious interactions with the handsome

Lazio had been of the innocent kind? Yet here she was: the proud mother of droopy-eared Delice and her brother, Divanti.

Ah yes, Delice…You may remember our doggy monk was to be reincarnated in her form. Indeed, the same soul was now lying in the grass in Sweden, marveling at the love he – no, she felt for her mother, and feeling marvelously sprightly and content (if a little hungry). "I guess I could stay a while," she thought, as her eyes grew heavy and she yawned wide.

The human family's delight about the new arrivals was mixed with bewilderment, as they realized the size of their puppy cohort. "Hmmmm," Delice thought to herself as she drifted into slumber, "fourteen other pups? Well, I had better instill some order here and make sure the others know who's the boss." And with a satisfied grunt, she fell sound asleep. Within a week, Delice was the uncontested leader of the pack.

Not a day passed without mischief. One fine afternoon, whilst unobserved, Delice decided it was time for The Great Escape. Instructing her fourteen companions on how to break out of the puppy play area, she answered the call of the wild and led the dash towards the main road.

It was quite a sight: the family's daughter scrambling to recapture the tiny escape artists, who, of course, thought she had simply decided to join their escape!

That night, after all fifteen runaways had been safely returned to their little beds and were dreaming of great adventures, the family decided Delice was ready to embrace the world and join a new family.

At a Crossroads

Meanwhile, as peace settled over the farm and puppy dreams filled the air, 100 km eastbound, in the quaint town of Växjö, a young woman named Salla felt everything but peaceful. Her lifelong dream to live and work as an artist had finally grown so strong that she had left her career. She was vacillating between elation at taking control of her life and fears of stepping into the unknown. Old dreams and goals had also begun to bubble up to the surface.

That night, hunched over the computer, she found her fingers typing out one of those old dreams. She entered the words "Basset Griffon Vendeen puppies" into a search engine, wondering what it was about this breed that she liked so much. Was it the droopy ears, scruffy, bed-head look, or their stubborn nature? Funny, she thought to herself: at my age, people tend to think of marriage, parenthood, and security – and here I am, enrolled as a student again, seeking to break free of conventions, ready to unleash my creativity, and about to buy a dog!

As Salla snuggled into her covers later that night, she envisioned the next day's visit to the farm she had found online, where fifteen little puppies were waiting for a new home.

Little did she know that the reincarnated doggy monk in the body of a headstrong, moody hunting dog was about to become her guide and companion along life's twisty road.

First Encounter

The farm had a welcoming feel. After a quick exchange of pleasantries in the family's living room, it was time for the puppies to be introduced. As the door to the adjacent room opened, a wild flurry of action rushed in, barking, howling, whining, sniffing, running, climbing. Salla was overwhelmed by the energy and joie de vivre these little beings radiated… She wondered how to choose a companion from this crowd of overwhelming cuteness. Yet, as soon as the treats were spilled onto the floor, one particular puppy caught her attention: a puppy whose alert, independent manner, laser-focused search for treats, and insatiable appetite made her smile. This puppy - you may have already guessed it - was none other than Delice.

"We need to figure out a name for you," Salla mused over the sound of the car engine in her sing-song Finnish-Swedish accent, holding a trembling but excited Delice in her lap. "Delice is somewhat too precious for a little tomboy like you. How about *Feliz*, which means *happy* in Spanish?"

"Oh boy," Delice thought to herself, "does this mean I'm going to have to put on a jolly dog act for the rest of my life?" She sighed inwardly and mustered her best adorable-puppy-dog look.

Finding First Routines

The following morning it was time to establish shared routines. "Aahhh, routines..." Feliz exclaimed to herself, "how we dogs love a structured day!" While Salla slipped into her rain boots, Feliz remembered her monk teacher, who emphasized that the beauty of routines lay in noticing and appreciating changes in one's surroundings and within oneself.

Outside, neither Salla nor Feliz noticed the cold drizzle sweeping across from the West. It was only when they stood outside the local dog park that she jolted back to reality.

"Did Salla really think a proud hunting dog like my good self was going to hang around the local gossip hounds?" Feliz glanced skeptically at the mix of canine beings checking her out."

I think this will be what Julius Cesar would have referred to as a *veni, vidi, vici* moment," she thought, as she made her nonchalant entrance into the park.

On their second morning, Salla rolled out her old bike from the garage, imagining how much fun it would be to ride down the lakeside path with her new companion.

"Are you kidding me?" Feliz scoffed privately. "I thought we were clear about our morning routines! Do you really expect me to run alongside a bike, like in some dog food commercial, stumbling over my long, floppy Basset ears?!" Yet, before a paw could be set down in protest, off they went.

A few kilometers down the shore, just as Salla was beginning to relax and enjoy the ride, a rabbit crossed their path. Instantly, Feliz's hunting instincts kicked in. She bounded after her prey, yanking the leash and pulling Salla and the bike into the bushes. The rabbit darted away, disappearing in the thicket.

"So much for proving my hunting prowess," grumbled Feliz, without explicitly blaming the clumsy novice by her side. Covered in mud, Salla struggled up from the ground, equally peeved by the abrupt interruption of her breezy ride. Yet, neither of them held a grudge, and soon they trundled on. "I guess we need to work out our priorities," Salla ventured. "Exactly!" Feliz agreed.

The Artist Dog Takes Center Stage

After several bruises and bent bike wheels, the two of them finally agreed that forest walks and occasional jogs were the winner regarding daily routines. They spent afternoons painting in the studio, a small room with a bright red wall that Salla had converted into her own creative space.

Nestled in a corner of the room, surrounded by an ocean of paint bottles, was a comfortable bed from which Feliz could nod her approval of Salla's ongoing work. The creative vibes became so contagious that Feliz developed an itch to contribute…

One afternoon, lazing in her studio bed, she started planning her first piece. "Hmm, I wonder if anyone's done a rainbow-colored paw print? Or an abstract portrait of my nemesis, the neighbor's cat?"

Whilst fantasizing about the fame and glamor she would inevitably attain, the wise words of her old teacher echoed in her mind: "Remember Monks, true success is not ego-based. True success comes out of the ability to remain centered in the moment and not let your thoughts interfere."

"Hmm...," Feliz thought as she looked up at Salla, who was struggling with a composition, "I wonder how I could pass on this knowledge to Salla? That girl definitely needs to start trusting the universe and stop controlling every step of her creative process!"

Incessant Doing

Although the two companions enjoyed some moments of tranquility, it was evident that Feliz's mission to lead Salla toward a state of inner peace was going to require training. Not a week passed without midweek dinner parties, girls' nights with red wine and midnight munchies, weekend sailing trips and/or elaborate costume parties.

Though Feliz embraced the hustle and bustle and liked being center stage, her old wise soul could see how this restlessness kept Salla from listening inward and finding her own truth.

Deep down, Salla knew, too, that although business suits had given way to colorful tops, and salary slips to student loans, these changes were merely on an external level.

How did one find greater meaning in life? Lasting contentedness and a feeling of equanimity from which to live and create? Unsure about where to begin, she figured revisiting her past could be a good place to start.

Revisiting the Past

The magic of the place was palpable, as Salla and Feliz slowly rolled up the hill to an old timber house tucked into a dark, misty spruce forest. "So, this is where the renowned mystic and regressive hypnotist lived," Salla thought, as she stood on the porch, gingerly knocking on the wooden door.

Salla was welcomed in and guided into the living room where her past life was to unfold. Meanwhile, Feliz glimpsed through the window to see what this mystical place was all about. Hanging

from the ceiling were puppets of all shapes and sizes, dangling down as if engaged in a shamanic dance.

So mesmerized was she by the sight that she failed to notice a cat had snuck up on her. Before she knew it, she had been drawn into its hypnotic wizard gaze.

As eager as you may be, dear reader, to uncover their past lives, we remain outside the window with Feliz, catching only a glimpse. The full story – a return to Salla's true love in 18ᵗʰ-century Britain – will fill the pages of another book.

Connecting with the Universe

Spring came early that year, along with an explosion of wild rabbits in the backyard. One typical afternoon, as Salla was painting and Feliz reveled in chasing bunnies through the window, Salla decided to put on a calming CD with meditative chants sung by doggy monks.

What happened then took both of them by surprise: as the first note echoed through the studio, Feliz's entire body froze. Then, much to her own surprise, she heard herself responding from the depths of her heart, with an enormous, deep, wolf-like howl.

Suddenly it all came flooding back: waves of memories from her past life washed over her... Images of her teachers and monk friends in their peaceful valley far, far away... Oh, how she missed them in that moment!

Salla, shocked by the intensity of Feliz's reaction, hurried to stop the music, but it wasn't until she took Feliz up into her lap that she was able to calm down her canine friend.

From that day on Salla knew she had no ordinary dog. Perhaps Feliz had indeed sung these beautiful chants in a previous life. They began to meditate together, sitting side by side, Feliz connecting with her dog ancestors and Salla hoping for a break from her restless mind.

Their shared life had slowly begun to take shape. While they loved the beautiful routines and fun diversions, they could not anticipate what lay waiting around the corner. To Salla's and Feliz's astonishment, their real adventure was only about to start.

A Big Thank You

To Meggie George for your amazing work at setting the narrative pace and tone, to Jonathan for contributing with your witty humor, to Viki for your patience and professionalism and to all the people following the story online who encouraged me to complete the book.

About the Author

Sanna Myrttinen is a visual artist born in 1973, in Helsinki, Finland. After an international education and career, she now lives and works in Starnberg, Southern Germany. Her works are exhibited regularly in galleries and at shows across Europe. Her painting studio lies on a farm in the beautiful Bavarian countryside. "The Adventures of Feliz" is her first book series.

About the Series

The idea for the series evolved as the author's first dog, Feliz, at the grand age of 16, left the Earthly realms to rejoin her dog ancestors. The series is a celebration of her life and of their many adventures together.

In the series, Feliz, a former dog monk, is reborn onto Earth to accompany a young woman on her road to a more meaningful and happy life. Although Feliz is filled with wisdom and tends to be spiritually a step ahead of her new human companion, she too has her own challenges and quirks to overcome. Their adventures take them from the Arctic Sea to the Southern tip of Italy and from life lessons learnt from nature to those of ancient sages. The series is as much a geographical and spiritual journey, as it is one of two friends on their path to a life of joy, meaning and inner peace.

CPSIA information can be obtained
at www.ICGtesting.com
Printed in the USA
BVHW040951080721
611454BV00010B/126